MentHER

Guide for Entrepreneurs

By Alicia Syrett

Dedication

This book is dedicated to all the amazing women who took the first step and began the entrepreneurial journey. You are the role models who will inspire the next generation of women who will follow in your footsteps.

Acknowledgments

Thank you to my business partners, Diana Murakhovskaya and Irene Ryabaya, who worked tirelessly with me to make #MentHERnyc a reality.

Thanks to all our panelists, Mentors, and the CNBC team for generously giving their time and advice to our women entrepreneurs and for contributing directly to the diversity of the NYC startup ecosystem.

Thanks to all the Contributors whose guidance and inspirational quotes can be found throughout this guide:

Nisa Amoils	Tracy Chadwell	Meghan Cross
Olu Fajemirokun-Beck	Katie Frankel	Elizabeth Galbut
Anna Garcia	Alex Goldberg	Hillary Gosher
Nimi Katragadda	Sacha Levy	Mary Liu
Lylan Masterman	Jessica Peltz-Zatulove	Adam Quinton
Barbara Raho	Larry Richenstein	Barbara Roberts
Jeff Seltzer	Jeffrey Silverman	Brett Topche
Stephanie Weiner		

Finally, thank you to Elizabeth Galbut for designing the cover of this Guide. I love it!

Contents

"Love what you do. You will be doing it a long time."

Barbara Roberts, The New York Angels

Introduction

Congratulations on all your success thus far! Most people never have the courage to take the first step, and you've done it. There is still a challenging journey ahead, but we hope to help you by providing helpful tips in this Guide for Entrepreneurs.

You're used to working harder. You're used to being scrutinized. But you got this. There is a community behind you pulling for you. You're part of a movement, and you're changing the world for the better.

Good luck and best wishes! You are going to be great.

1. Tips for Women in Business

    1. Use charm and laughter. Women are inherently very powerful. We can command a room when we want to. Don't let biases get the best of you or make you angry.

    2. Dress the part and power pose. My father used to tell me, "Dress how you want to be treated," and I think there's truth to that. Also be aware of your body language by not crossing your arms and holding a defensive stance.

    3. Be proactive. Get out there and be a thought leader. Organize events, write posts, and connect people. Build a brand and attract people to you.

    4. Demand transparency and be vocal when diversity is lacking. Speak up when you see an all-male panel or all-male leadership team. Support others who speak out too. We have to make it clear that diversity is the norm.

    5. Save the word "sorry" for only your closest relationships when you really mean it. Watch out for words that diminish your power or credibility like "sorry" or "just" in a business setting.

    6. Where you sit is where you stand. Don't marginalize yourself by sitting in the back where you go unseen and

unheard. I recommend going right for the middle at the table!

7. Recommend women for opportunities. Constantly think of ways you can support other women. If you can't make an event, suggest a woman in your place. If you can make an event, ask if you can help recommend other women to attend too.

8. Give to get. Take time to share what you've learned with other women. By helping, it will likely come back to you in a positive way. I believe in karma.

9. Constantly ask for things. The worst thing someone can do is tell you "no," and then you're no better off than where you started. Ask for advice, suggestions, and feedback.

10. Anchor high in negotiations. Know that the end point of negotiations often end as an average of where you and the other side start. Don't disadvantage yourself by starting with a fair proposal if the other side is starting with a proposal that strongly favors their position. Anchor high so that if you give on a negotiation point here or there, you're not giving up major ground.

2. Don't Forget The Important Things in Life

When you're on your entrepreneurial journey, don't forget to take care of yourself:

1. Sleep well, eat healthy, and exercise.

2. Make time for friends, family, and love.

3. Listen to music, dance, and travel.

4. Learn and enrich yourself with events and experiences.

Practical Tips for Entrepreneurs

3. What Should I Put In A Pitch Deck?!?

    Putting together a pitch deck is so important. It can make or break a relationship with a potential investor. If it's too long, the investor may lose interest. If it's too short, the investor may think that the entrepreneur hasn't done his or her diligence. So what's the best approach?

    Listed below are the key components of any pitch deck. They are essentially the major topics that a smart investor will eventually cover in a due diligence process. Most entrepreneurs get only 10 minutes (if that!) to pitch their business in 10-15 slides, so if you address these topics comprehensively from the start, you're well on your way to piquing the investor's interest and getting the next meeting.

    So here goes...

    Business Summary – What does your business do? I can't say how many times an entrepreneur launches into a lengthy explanation about the problem he or she is solving and the size of the market only to have an investor raise their hand mid-presentation and say, "But what do you do?!?" Tell your audience what your business does clearly and succinctly from the start.

Market Assessment – How big is your market? Most investors want to know that you're playing in a multi-billion dollar market. That way, if you carve out even a small portion of the space, you can develop a multi-million dollar business. Do your research and demonstrate that the market is large and attractive.

Barriers to Entry – What's to prevent competitors from replicating your idea? Perhaps you have a patent which protects your technology or intellectual property which no one else possesses. Maybe you have exclusive relationships with partners or customers. Whatever your edge is, investors want to understand your competitive advantage.

Scalability – How does your business scale? Scalability is the difference between investing in one doctor launching an individual practice and investing in a software company which all doctors with practices can purchase. Investors want to understand how your business can grow, geographically and/or across a large customer base, by making the most of limited resources.

Traction – What milestones have you reached to date? This could mean a number of things. You could highlight revenues generated, users acquired, strategic partners, etc. Whatever your metrics, investors want to see that you've made progress and are demonstrating proof that your concept will be successful.

Sales and Marketing – How are you reaching your audience? Perhaps you plan to build out a sales team. Maybe you have a social media plan or established partnerships to help acquire users. Investors want to know how you intend to reach your audience, and many want to understand whether you have thought through the costs required to obtain customers.

Team – What are the backgrounds of your team? Maybe you have deep expertise in the sector, or maybe someone on your team is developing the software. Investors want to understand why you and your team are best positioned to make the company successful. If you're a serial entrepreneur who has sold a company in the past, you know to highlight that too!

Competition – Who are your competitors and how do you compare to them? A matrix can be helpful here in neatly displaying all the major players in the space (including you!) and how each measures up across different criteria. (Hint: you will likely have more checks against the criteria while your competitors have more x's!).

Exit Strategy – How are investors going to get a return on their money? Be thoughtful about who could potentially acquire your company and what comparable transactions have occurred in your space. Investors do not want to invest in "lifestyle businesses" where they will never get their money back. It is critical that investors and entrepreneurs be in agreement on this topic from the start so that they are working towards the same exit goals throughout the growth of the business.

Funding Needs – How much are you raising and what is the structure of the offering? It helps to be clear not only about the total funds needed but also how those funds will be spent. Are you spending money on hires, technology, marketing, etc.? Also, be clear about whether you are offering convertible debt or equity, how you are valuing your company, and any relevant legal terms of the offering.

Financials – What are the past financials and future projections of your company? Some companies seek funding before revenues are generated while others may have already generated sales. In any case, investors want to see relevant metrics (e.g. sales, expenses, gross margins, etc.) for historical periods, if applicable, and future projections going forward.

And there you have it! The above topics make a great pitch deck, and it goes without saying that the overall presentation should also be of high quality. But there's one more critical component...PASSION!!! Investors want to see entrepreneurs with enthusiasm. Make sure your oral delivery of the pitch deck conveys the same excitement and drive which inspired you to found the company in the first place, and you should be well on your way!

4. Do's and Don'ts in Pitching

DO...

1. Explain your business model and exactly how you make money. This includes addressing pricing, costs, and margins. We need to understand the economics of solving this problem or serving a need.

2. Tell us why YOU are the best team to make this happen. We want to know your backgrounds and areas of expertise. We need to understand why we would bet on you vs. any other players in the space.

3. Address your competitive edge, which can include intellectual property, patent protection, and exclusive relationships. We need to understand what prevents others from replicating what you're doing.

4. Give us a sense of traction achieved and milestones reached to date. This includes revenues generated, units sold, customers acquired, awards and accolades, and strategic alliances.

5. Give us insight into your customer. This includes their demographic, how you've branded your product for them, the cost of acquiring them, their experience with your product or service, and frequency of use.

6. Talk about your long term vision for the company including growth plans for future products and geographic markets. If you're raising money, we also need to know the terms and your 'exit strategy' for return on capital.

7. Explain how your business scales. We want to know that this is more than just a niche opportunity. Say how you grow across a large customer base in various geographies while making the most of limited resources.

8. Talk about your sales and marketing plan for acquiring customers. For example, this could include salespeople,

partnerships, social media, promotions, customer referrals, events, and loyalty programs.

DON'T...

1. Say that there's no competition...there's always competition! Not addressing this can make you sound naïve, and future players can always enter your market. Be thoughtful and state how you can position yourself to win.

2. Launch into a long story about the customer's problem, the market, or your team without first *clearly and succinctly stating what you do.* If you don't do that from the start, you've already lost our attention.

3. Overestimate the size of your market. You want to operate in a multi-billion dollar market, but you don't want to say that you're attacking a $100 billion market when you're really only addressing a smaller part of it.

4. Do a "top-down" instead of "bottoms-up" market analysis! Saying that you'll capture 1% of a $100 billion market is

too simplistic. Walk us through unit sales and how they add up market by market as you grow.

5. Forget to address any relevant legal issues and risks. We would never want to be blindsided by a government action or customer lawsuit. Help us understand the potential risks and how you're addressing them.

6. Be too salesy! Be honest and authentic. Support your claims with facts, research, and data, and independently measure your results. If something sounds too good to be true to us, we know it probably is!

7. Forget to address seasonality or cyclicality of your product or industry. We need to understand the volatility of sales and customer behavior so that we aren't surprised by unexpected changes in results.

8. Forget to show passion and deliver a great presentation! It's all about the entrepreneur after all, and we want to believe in

"When you're presenting your company to a room full of investors; it's easier to be intimidated by the power play of immediate cash they have versus the long term equity you can provide. The thing to keep in mind is that you're the expert. You live and breathe your company, so you yourself are the educated, credible source for the domain you're benefiting, the behavior you're changing, or the functionality you're inventing. When you're speaking to potential investors, use a similar tone you would for your family or friends; guide them through the market opportunity by educating them rather than pitching. But at the same time, educate; don't alienate. Expect investors to ask some questions that to you seem obvious, and be excited to address them with your informed explanation."

Meghan Cross, Red Bear Angels

you! Ideas are a dime a dozen, but a dynamic entrepreneur who knows how to execute is pure gold!

"During a pitch you should state what your business/product is upfront. Too many times potential investors are at the end of your pitch still figuring out what you do."

Jeff Seltzer, Pierce Yates Ventures

5. Do's and Don'ts in Fundraising

   You've Perfected Your Pitch, Now What?!

   DOs and DON'Ts: Conquering the Fundraise!

   DO...

   1. Focus on finding local investors first! They can make helpful introductions to nearby contacts and are more available for face-to-face time. Be careful about chasing big investor names; they are solicited often, and the odds are much lower you'll catch their eye, especially when you have to travel to get their attention.

   2. Research investors before contacting them! Do your homework on them as they would on you. Talk to other entrepreneurs they've invested in for tips. Remember that your relationship with them may be 10 years or more (longer than the average marriage!), so fit matters!

   3. Be a thought leader! By speaking, writing, and organizing events actively in your start-up community, you can attract investors organically by demonstrating your depth of knowledge in your area of expertise.

4. Think of every meeting as an opportunity to advance your company with an investor generally, whether they invest or not! Investors are often highly influential and accomplished people. They may be helpful in spreading the word about you or sharing strategic opportunities.

5. Know the best funding structure for you! Investigate all the options (e.g. angels, VCs, loans, crowdfunding, etc.). It may not even make sense for you to offer equity in your company, so be sure about the right structure before you ask for money.

6. Make use of your alumni network! Your school and fellow alums want you to be successful, so reach out to them and ask for help. They may provide advice and introductions, and some may even decide to invest!

7. Remember that the process is always in your control! If you don't feel like the investor is the right fit for you, you don't have to proceed with conversations. By recognizing this early, you may save yourself critical time by avoiding unnecessary due diligence requests.

8. Involve your Advisors in fundraising! Bring them to meetings with you if it's helpful to project an image of gravitas. Involve them in the process by sharing information and updates so that they have a chance to pitch in and help you succeed.

DON'T...

1. Expect a check at the end of a first meeting! Due diligence processes often take weeks or months of exchanging information. Focus on building a relationship with the investor. You want to make sure that this is someone you can potentially work with for a decade.

2. Send cold emails! Get a warm introduction though a trusted contact. Most investors are inundated with random solicitations, so your cold email will likely be deleted. An introduction from a close connection will set you apart and increase your chances of getting attention and being funded.

3. Expect investors to respond during holidays! Investors often travel with their families in late December/early January period,

and many don't hold meetings during August at all. Time your contact so that you have their full attention.

4. Post controversial content on social media! Savvy investors are always looking for red flags and reasons not to fund you. If you share content which contains negative, incendiary information, you can kiss that check goodbye.

5. Think money solves all your problems! Pouring lots of money into a bad idea just delays the ultimate result of the business not surviving. Plus, bootstrapping breeds creativity. Make sure you've proven the concept first. Show how you'll spend the money wisely in supercharging existing growth.

6. Be slow to respond to due diligence requests! Anticipate the questions that investors will ask and have all your documents ready. This will speed up your fundraising process and ensure investors that you are organized and responsive.

7. Be discouraged if the initial answer is NO! If an investor declines to fund you, they haven't necessarily rejected you

---

"Look for investors who can add value with more than just capital."

Katie Frankel, ff Venture Capital

---

forever! You can make progress on their feedback and revisit the opportunity to speak with them at a later date.

8. Forget that you're competing with all other entrepreneurs who are currently fundraising! Be honest with yourself about how attractive your start-up is vs. others, and make sure you proceed when you truly believe you'll stand out from the crowd.

6. Length of Time for a Fundraise

How long does it take to fundraise? It depends! It could take a few weeks to multiple months depending on the following factors:

- The experience of the entrepreneur. If you've raised money before, it's much easier. You're a "serial entrepreneur" and you can anticipate diligence requests and rely on relationships you've already built.

- The time of year of the raise. Investors are generally not active in August or in the late December/early January time period. Time your raise accordingly. The periods from September-December, January-April, and May-July are good targets.

- The demand for the round. If there is already momentum in your raise (i.e. you've obtained a lead investor or there isn't much room left in your round), it's much easier to keep the momentum going and close the round.

- The relative attractiveness of other entrepreneurs pitching at the time. If you're presenting to an angel group, they may see 10 companies throughout the course of a morning. Know your relative attractiveness vs. other entrepreneurs in the market so that you also know how to stand out.

- What's going on in the broader economy. High net worth investors can be spooked when there is equity market turmoil or macro events which create uncertainty. Be attuned to this and time your ask accordingly. It's harder to ask investors to allocate money to long-term, illiquid investments when the markets are volatile.

"You only get one first impression—your elevator pitch is that first impression, so make it count."

Katie Frankel, ff Venture Capital

7. Presenting to an Angel Network

- Be aware of the group's seasonality of activity. Most angel groups don't hold meetings in the late December/early January holiday period or in August. Plan accordingly!

- Do your diligence on the group before applying. Talk to the entrepreneurs from the group's portfolio companies and ask them about the process for tips. Research the members' backgrounds for potential fit with your company. Look for alumni connections. Know which members actively and regularly lead deals and seek out warm introductions.

- If a member has recommended you apply to the group, don't forget to cite their name when submitting your application! It definitely helps.

- Have your diligence items ready. If you anticipate which questions will be asked and keep all the files in a handy location, you can speed up your diligence process by responding quickly in an organized way.

- Don't think of pitching as a binary outcome (i.e. you get funded or get rejected). If the group declines to proceed with your company, they haven't rejected you forever! You can make progress on their comments and revisit the opportunity to pitch with them at a later date. Don't be discouraged if the initial answer is no.

- When you pitch, remember that there are a lot of highly influential and accomplished people in the room. Even if you don't have the opportunity continue the process into due diligence, think of the pitch as a great chance to tell a group of movers and shakers about your company. They may be helpful in just communicating with others about you and/or thinking about strategic opportunities that may be relevant for you.

- Consider including an "ask" in your pitch which might also be attractive to the group's members. For example, if you think there may be members who could serve on your Advisory Board, mention that too as it may provide an opportunity for you to start a relationship with angels and receive strategic advice, regardless of whether they choose to invest or not.

- The process is always in your control. If the due diligence process doesn't feel right to you or you don't think the members are a fit for your company, you don't have to proceed.

8. Was It Something I Said? Angel Pet Peeves to Avoid!

Was that a groan you just heard in the audience while presenting? A snicker, perhaps? Or maybe you just sensed that you lost credibility in some way. You've worked so hard on your business and conveying the opportunity to potential investors is so important to you, so how do you avoid some common pitfalls which frustrate angels?

Here are a few angel pet peeves to avoid…

There's no competition! – Of course there's competition! There's always competition. I once heard someone say that before OpenTable, the competition was a paper and pen. And there's potential for future competition too. There's always the possibility that a large company with deep pockets replicates what you're doing. Saying there's no competition can sound naïve; however, addressing the competitive landscape thoughtfully and honestly while showing how you can persevere regardless is a smart move.

That's not your market! – Be careful about citing market statistics. For example, you could tell your audience that the travel industry is $100+ billion dollar market, but the vast majority of this spend represents what people pay for flights. So, unless you're proposing to start a new airline and compete with the likes of

American Airlines, Delta, etc., that's not your market! Be specific about your actual market. If you're proposing to create a service to lead consumers to last-minute flights, then perhaps it's more realistic to look at the *marketing spend* of airlines in particular as your potential market may be what airlines pay to attract consumers to purchase a flight, and that market is much smaller, albeit still attractive.

And if we only capture 1% of this market...we'll make a billion dollars! – Use bottoms up not top down analysis. What does that mean? If you're producing widgets, don't just say that 1% of the widget market equal x billions of dollars. Do the homework. Demonstrate the demand for your product. Show the revenue and costs per widget. Show how the widget sales growth occurs market by market and how you scale the business. Let investors see the growth on a unit by unit basis so that – in aggregate and over time – it is clear how you actually capture 1% of the market in practice.

Finally, don't be too salesy! You know the saying "if something's too good to be true, it probably is"? Well, if you're pitching to an intelligent audience, you shouldn't need to sell too hard. Be authentic. Be honest. Establish trust. Use facts and research to support your case. The data should speak for you and paint a much more compelling picture.

> *"Most investors are very public – know their opinions from blog posts, know what stage they invest in, if they lead, what check size they write, and if they've invested in your space (or in your competitors!). Coming prepared to the conversation goes a long way, and ensures a more productive discussion versus a 'pitch'."*

Jessica Peltz-Zatulove, kbs+ Ventures

You want to be optimistic (you're an entrepreneur after all!), but you also want investors to believe that you are pragmatic and really understand what it takes to make your dream a reality. And it doesn't hurt to avoid the angel pet peeves cited above to convince others you're a savvy entrepreneur. Good luck with your pitch!

9. Diligencing an Investor

    Before you approach a potential investor, you must do your homework! All too often, entrepreneurs reach out to a recognizable name without first doing simple research to determine whether the investor is a fit. Consider the following before you attempt to make contact:

    - Level of Involvement: How involved does this investor become with their investments? Does that fit what you're looking for in terms of an active vs. passive investor? What have they done for their portfolio companies in the past? Are you comfortable with the frequency of their communication and the extent they ask for information and feedback?

    - Industry Focus: Does this investor invest in your industry? Do they possess a depth of knowledge in your space to be able to offer useful advice?

    - Geographical Focus: Where are the companies based in which they invest? Some investors only focus locally, some regionally, some nationally, and some globally. Make sure they consider investments in your geography before reaching out.

"Keep in mind taking money from an investor is more binding than a marriage- choose wisely! I always recommend that the founder does as much diligence on the investor as the investors will do on them. The most telling sign is to talk to founders- ask to speak to a few founders in the portfolio that have succeeded, and also a few that have failed- that's when you can really better understand the character and temperament of the investor. Given the ups and downs of startups, you have to create a supportive investors community where you're comfortable being transparent and potentially vulnerable with, it's inevitably going to be a bumpy ride."

Jessica Peltz-Zatulove, kbs+ Ventures

- Check Size: What size checks do they typically write? Is their range or typical amount consistent with what you're seeking for your round?

- Valuation: What is their valuation focus? Does their valuation preference fit with your current valuation?

10. Being Diligenced as an Entrepreneur

    Before I go on CNBC's PowerPitch, I take a couple of hours to do diligence on the entrepreneur and company. Note that I said the *entrepreneur* and company as I believe the person (and their team) is the most important part of the equation. Here is some of the basic ground I cover:

- The Entrepreneur: I look through their Twitter and Facebook feeds. I check for connections on LinkedIn and reach out to anyone we have in common to get feedback. I'm looking for red flags! If you're posting something nasty about your ex or your content is offensive and controversial, I'm staying away.

- The Company: I look through the company website. I download and play with the app, if applicable. I go through the company's social media: Facebook, Twitter, Instagram, Pinterest, LinkedIn, YouTube. I search for the company in Crunchbase, AngelList, and Gust. I try to find a pitch deck. I search for the company in the Better Business Bureau, on Amazon and on Kickstarter and pay close attention to customer reviews and complaints.

- My checklist: I cross-reference everything I see with my own checklist for what should be in a pitch deck. I zero in on some of the main areas (e.g. competitive advantage, sales and marketing strategy, etc.) that may not be addressed. I show up prepared and ready to dig into specific questions where information is lacking, not to be pitched to or educated on the business for the first time.

*"Take as much advice as possible and never stop asking
for it. Take as little money as possible until you've got
paying customers. Advisors are free and can be highly
valuable. Investors are very expensive and can be highly
variable".*

Hilary Gosher, Insight Venture Partners

Q&A

- How do I position myself if I'm a wife/husband or
  sister/brother team?

  This is a tough one because some investors are adamantly
  against investing in these types of teams. With that said,
  many investors are open to it. For investors that are
  undecided, you need to be prepared to give a compelling
  answer as to why this is not an issue. I recommend citing
  examples of successful exits (e.g. Michael and Kass Lazerow of
  Buddy Media, Diane Greene and Mendel Rosenblum of VM
  Ware, etc.) as proof that this can be a positive trait.

- How much should I offer an Advisor in equity and how should
  it vest?

  It depends! Specifically, it depends on the notoriety of the
  potential Advisor and how involved you anticipate they will
  be. I've seen ranges from 0.10% to several percentage points
  of the company. Most agreements seem to be 0.25% or
  maybe 0.50% (if the Advisor is well known and has a track
  record of being active). I recommend a vesting structure of 4
  equal increments where ¼ vests immediately and the
  remaining ¼'s vest over the next 3 years. You have to decide
  what works best for you. Additionally, if the Advisor is also an

investor, you might consider offering them an amount of Advisor equity that increases as their investment increases (e.g. if they invest $10k they also receive 0.10% Advisor equity, if they invest $50k they also receive 0.50% Advisor equity).

- What other forms of financing exist beyond offering equity?

   It may never make sense to sell equity to outside investors! If you sell equity to outside investors, they will need to get their money back at some point via an exit (likely the sale of your company). If you're not looking to give up control, there are many types of non-dilutive funding such as small business loans, grants, revenue-based financing, crowdfunding, and customer pre-payments which may make a lot more sense for a business to pursue instead of or prior to offering equity. Do the research and figure out what's best for you.

- What do I do when I get conflicting advice from Mentors and Investors?

   Ah, you're describing Mentor Whiplash! Don't worry, it happens all the time. For example, I've told you in this guide to address Exit Strategy in your pitch deck and to use a grid in mapping out the competitive space because I believe most investors prefer this. However, any individual investor might disagree! The key is to do your research. Read about each potential investor, listen to their podcasts, go hear them speak, and tailor your pitch accordingly. Similarly, you may get conflicting strategic advice from Mentors. That's okay too. Be appreciative and give it all consideration, and then decide what's best for you and your company.

- How do you recommend dealing with biased investors?

Unfortunately, there are a number of negative players in the industry with entrenched biases. I try not to deal with them if possible and to instead direct my attention and efforts to fulfilling my goals and helping others who reflect my values and beliefs. My best advice to you is to first do your research and ask around to other entrepreneurs. They will likely tell you who to avoid. No money is worth dealing with someone with these issues. And if you meet someone and they turn out to be a bad apple, make sure to warn others when asked to save them time.

- What metrics/KPIs does an investor want to see?

It depends on the type of business you have! It could be revenues generated, users acquired, customer churn, recurring purchases, cost to acquire a customer, time spent on a platform, etc. The key is to do your research and find the relevant metrics for your business and industry and then be prepared with your own data.

- What's the difference fundraising in NYC vs. Silicon Valley?

The general stereotype is that money has been more free flowing in Silicon Valley with higher valuations and investors more willing to bet on a vision vs. New York where the business model and traction matter more. Like so many other areas, you have to do your diligence on individuals and specific firms to tailor your approach, no matter where they are based.

- What's the difference between a product vs. an investment pitch?

A product pitch focuses mainly on the details of the product whereas an investment pitch focuses on the business as a whole. For example, in an investment pitch, there will likely be a slide or two describing the product, but there will also be many slides addressing the business (e.g. financials, financing, sales and marketing, market, etc.). When fundraising, don't make the mistake of only focusing on the product. A potential investor needs and wants to understand the dynamics of the business holistically.

- Do I want active or passive investors, or both?

   Likely both! It's great to have active investors who are constantly there for you, and it's also great to have investors who write checks and trust you to run the business completely. It's like a barbell structure. Beware of the investor that falls somewhere in between who is not regularly in the information flow yet pops in and out of the picture and makes many demands on your time which distract you from running the business.

- What role does press play in fundraising?

   Press can be helpful in fundraising. It can serve as a validation that there is interest in your company from the broader market. It can also help spread the word to potential customers which could convert to sales. However, press can be ephemeral. It may be nice but may not move your core metrics. It's generally positive but it's not necessarily a sign that you've made the big time! Investors know to take it with a grain of salt.

- What's the ideal level of contact from investors?

In an ideal world, I would say that you stay in contact with active investors on a regular basis (e.g. emails or phone calls every 2-3 weeks). It should be a virtuous cycle in that the more information you share, the more investors can help, the more investors help, the more you want to share, etc. With that said, there may be times when you are in frequent contact daily and other times when there is nothing to discuss for weeks or months. For best practices, I would recommend entrepreneurs maintain discipline and proactively share a monthly or quarterly update with all investors (regardless of their level of communication with each of them individually).

- If it were you, what would you do?

If it were me, I would probably never raise outside equity! I would definitely have an Advisory Board though. I recommend bootstrapping as long as you can; it spurs creativity. Fundraising also takes a lot of time. I recommend raising outside equity if/when your business model is proven and - although you are in a good position without it - raising equity to supercharge your growth. Don't forget to investigate all the non-dilutive forms of equity before embarking on your fundraising journey.

<u>Running Your Company</u>

11. How Can an Advisory Board Help?

   Active investors and helpful Advisors can be more valuable to a business than money at times. So what can you ask of your Advisory Board and/or what are best practices of things great Advisors do? Read below for some ideas!

   1. Making introductions across strategic areas. Great Advisors open up their network to you and help you in almost any area of need. They can introduce you to other investors, potential employees, potential partners, accountants, lawyers, etc. You have to keep them apprised of your needs regularly so that they know how to help.

   2. Sending articles of interest. Attentive Advisors keep you in mind while reviewing any information that comes their way. They can share articles related to new funds/investors in your industry, competitive activity, and sales leads, amongst other areas.

3. Helping fundraise. In addition to introducing you to other investors, an active Investor/Advisor can potentially lead your fundraise by setting the terms, writing a deal memo, and herding other investors through the process.

4. Helping recruit other members of your Advisory Board. Introductions are not only relevant to your daily business needs. If there are specific knowledge voids you'd like to fill (e.g. legal perspective, exit experience, etc.), they may be able to recruit other members to join them on your Board.

5. Helping in the recruiting process. In addition to making introductions, Advisors can also interview potential candidates. They may be able to offer a knowledgeable yet somewhat unbiased and distanced perspective which could be additive in your hiring process.

6. Attending strategic meetings with you. When your company is small, taking an Advisor to an important meeting with you can project added gravitas and credibility.

7. Helping you get press. Great Advisors are also often active in the startup community. They can leverage their own influence and network to help you obtain interviews, speaking engagements, and media coverage.

8. Serving as a reference. Once you've built a relationship with an Advisor, they can turn to you to offer another perspective on your leadership when critical deals need to be closed and references are requested.

"Sales ability is key for entrepreneurs. You need to be able to sell your idea to investors so they will fund your business; you need to sell to your management team so they will share your vision and enthusiasm and propel your business forward; and you always have to sell to your customer or you don't have a business at all."

Barbara Raho, Golden Seeds

12. Sales & Marketing = Salespeople & Social Media, Right?!?

'Sales and Marketing' is integral to any business and is certainly one of the key topics in any pitch deck. Yet, I often see startups gloss over the subject without giving it the attention it truly deserves. Or worse, they make the assumption that it does not need to be addressed because they will just go viral! While it is a possibility that your product or service is so good that clients beat down the door to buy from you, the vast majority of time it takes a thoughtful approach to communicating with potential customers.

Having worked with a number of startups over time, I've compiled a list of 'Sales and Marketing' questions that I often use for the purposes of brainstorming with them to generate new ideas on potential tactics. I've shared them below in the hopes that they might spark some discussion amongst you and your team. Of course, many may not be applicable to your particular company, but isn't it better to 'check the box' or decide they are 'not applicable' instead of not thinking through it at all?!?

So here we go...

- Are **promotions or discounts** applicable to your product or service? If so, have you made use of them to drive sales? Are there certain times a year when they might be especially relevant to you?

- Is there a way to create **contests or competitions** to engage users or clients? Are there incentives you can add to encourage participation or ways you could incorporate '**gamification**' to drive desired behaviors?

- Are there mutually beneficial **partnerships** that you could pursue? Could another company's distribution network help spread the word about your product or service? Could you co-brand with another company to gain credibility, access or attention?

- Do you have current clients or users who are already big fans, and could you promote them as your **brand ambassadors** so that they are essentially marketing on your behalf? Are there **influencers** like bloggers or celebrities who are familiar with you, and can you leverage their reach?

- Can you host **events or experiences** where you engage with current and potential users directly? Could you bring key players in the industry to you via these events and brand yourself as a hub for industry intelligence in the process?

- Do you have unique information which gives you insights that you can share to portray yourself as a thought leader in your space and thus drive inquiries to you? Is there original **content** (e.g. blogs, top ten lists or rankings, data analytics, etc.) that you can produce which serves as a reason to reach out to current and potential clients?

- Are you soliciting feedback from current and potential clients? Could you use '**crowdsourcing**' as a means to engage these parties' participation to drive sales or develop leads?

- Have you thought about a **loyalty programs** or cross-selling opportunities which could drive additional sales with existing users or clients? Are there ways to create a feeling of **scarcity or exclusivity** within your incentive programs to drive sales?

- Have you thought comprehensively beyond sales professionals and social media to see if there are any unique outreach opportunities in radio, TV, catalogues, publications, billboards, etc.? Are you thinking about other **less obvious outlets or venues** to spread your message?

Of course, this is by no means a comprehensive list, but it may be helpful to start the conversation. And yes, you probably need to hire a salesperson at some point and get on social media too!

13. Best Practices for Board Meetings

When you're in the early stages of your company, you don't necessarily need all the Board formalities of a large company. With that said, here are some best practices I recommend:

- Hold meetings every 6 weeks or so. Your company's changing fast, so you likely want to meet more than once per quarter. You may even want to meet monthly. Schedule the meetings in advance and make sure to work around holidays.

- Send out an agenda before the meeting. The Board members should arrive fully informed on the company's status. The meeting is not the time to go through basic updates and financials. Share all the information in advance and give them time to be thoughtful.

- Use the meeting to brainstorm about strategic challenges. Once everyone is assembled, use the meeting to discuss a few key strategic challenges. These are pros and cons of opportunities, risks that keep you up at night, and areas where they can help.

- The meeting should last around 2 hours. Keep the meeting focused and efficient. Board members should stay engaged (and off their phones) the whole time.

"Send out your board deck 7 days before the board meeting."

Lylan Masterman, White Star Capital

- End the meeting with a to-do list for investors and entrepreneurs. Make use of your incredible Board members. Ask for help in the course of the meeting and be clear about the follow up expected from all parties as well as the accompanying deadlines upon conclusion.

When You're Ready to Pay it Forward

14. I Want To Be An Angel Investor! Now What?

So you've seen Shark Tank, and you want to call the shots. Where to begin? Having started this journey myself some time ago, I can recommend a number of resources and bits of advice (which you may or may not find helpful!) to get you started on your journey.

First, I would highlight two books: "Angel Financing for Entrepreneurs" by Susan Preston and "Winning Angels" by David Amis and Howard Stevenson. Also revisit "What Do I Put In a Pitch Deck?!" for a useful due diligence checklist as you read and listen to pitches and "Angel Pet Peeves to Avoid" to detect red flags in entrepreneur presentations.

Now that you're armed with information, let's deal with practicalities...

Accredited Investor Status – Do a quick online search to see if you legally qualify to be an angel investor. This is risky stuff. These investments are illiquid, lack the transparency you see in the public markets, and have a higher rate of failure. Don't become an angel investor unless you are comfortable potentially losing money! Of course, there's potential to make a lot of money too, but you should only proceed if you legally qualify and are fully knowledgeable about the risk involved.

Will you be an active or passive investor?

Passive - If you're like most people, you have full time job! You may not be able to spend a lot of time on a daily basis with entrepreneurs, but you still may desire exposure to this asset class. If the idea of picking start-ups for your portfolio with minimal involvement afterwards and/or committing capital via lead investors who choose the startups appeals to you, then equity crowdfunding is a great place to start.

Equity Crowdfunding - There are a lot of websites which address this market: CircleUp, SeedInvest, AngelList, MicroVentures, etc. These sites allow you to register your profile and sort startups by sector and geography, amongst other criteria. You can invest in companies directly and/or invest in a syndicate (where a lead investor chooses the deals for you to create a diverse portfolio). Most platforms don't charge you for access, and they provide you with a lot of investment choices. They also streamline the investment process so that you can access many of the relevant company documents in one place and see what other investors think about the company.

Active – Two of the most important determinants of startup success from an angel's perspective are 1) the amount of time spent on due diligence before the investment and 2) the amount of time spent helping the company post-investment. If you have the time and inclination to be helpful to entrepreneurs, your guidance and advice will likely be well-received! Mentoring entrepreneurs can be incredibly fulfilling, but you should be prepared to be responsive, open your network to them, provide strategic advice, and participate in formal meetings (e.g. Board of Directors, Advisory Boards), if applicable. Active angels often join local angel networks to work on deals and invest together.

Angel Networks - Check out the Angel Capital Association's website for a member directory of angel groups in your region. Joining a local group gives you a sense of camaraderie with other angels, but more importantly, you can learn a lot by performing due diligence with your colleagues. Together, you can lead deals, negotiate investment terms, and work together with the company post-investment. Local networks often play a big role in the startup ecosystem too by providing guidance and feedback to entrepreneurs even before the fundraising process begins.

What else should I know?

Get a good lawyer! In all seriousness, no one enjoys paying legal bills, but a good lawyer is worth his/her weight in gold. Make sure you get solid advice from a trusted advisor before signing anything. Don't be penny wise and pound foolish as a little preparation now can really protect your interests in the long run. You should also make sure your accountant understands the tax ramifications and completes any filings necessary on your behalf.

But most importantly, don't forget to focus on the most important aspect of the investment decision: the entrepreneur! All too often, we can get enamored by a great idea, but if the entrepreneur isn't remarkable, the business may never take off. Plus, if you have a great relationship with the entrepreneur and believe in him/her, then you won't panic if/when the business pivots! Invest in the person and team. Put your money behind someone with incredible potential, and hopefully you become an integral part in making their dream a reality and building a spectacular business.

Appendix

Cissé Cocoa Company - Sample Pitch Deck

A special thanks to Diana Lovett, CEO of Cissé Cocoa Company, for providing the sample pitch deck below for your reference. Note that some areas (e.g. financials, exit strategy, funding needs) have been purposely redacted for confidentiality reasons. By the way, her products are absolutely as delicious as they look!

Cissé: goodies that taste good and do good too!

Cissé is a woman-owned cocoa company committed to using real, natural ingredients, sourced with care, to lovingly craft our ready-to-eat brownie thins and award-winning baking and hot cocoa mixes using a fully traceable supply chain.

How are we different: cocoa from bean to box

Cissé connects to customers in a personal way, enabling them to trace their cocoa from bean to box. Traceability is a step beyond Fair Trade and a compelling competitive differentiator.

Cissé is a pioneer– ensuring supply chain responsibility and disrupting the cocoa space by tying our reputation to our supply chain partners.

What do we do: our products

Super Thins
Crunchy, addictive ready-to-eat brownie thins

Baking Mixes
You'll never believe these came from a box!

Hot Cocoa Mixes
Award-winning cocoa mixes in beautiful gold canisters

4

Who supports us: our biggest fans

WSJ

"If we hadn't baked them ourselves, we never would have guessed that Cissé Trading Co.'s dark, dense, nearly molten double chocolate chip cookies come from a box..."

"Here on Sweets we don't need a reason to eat things like double chocolate chip muffins, but it's always nice to know that while indulging our sweet tooth, we're also helping change the world."

PBS

"Women-owned businesses are expected to lead the economic rebound... [and Cissé Trading Co. will] perhaps spur more women to turn a passion into a business venture."

THE
HUFFINGTON
POST

"The following three women not only started businesses that benefit the masses - offering healthier products, helping small farmers, and introducing innovative gluten-free foods - they also used their pregnancy and maternity leave to hone their big ideas and transform them into reality."

5

Where can you find us: 2000+ curated retailers

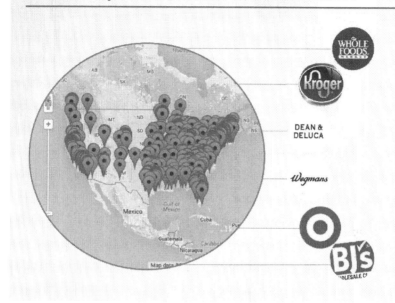

How have we grown distribution: exponentially!

Distribution growth over time (number of doors)

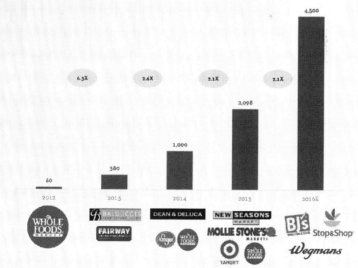

How did we get here: key milestones

March 2012
Successful meeting
with Whole Foods
North Atlantic

April 2012
Partnership with
FUNDOPO in the
Dominican Republic
established

September 2012
Cissé products hit
store shelves in 65
Whole Foods stores
and abesmarket.com

September 2013
Cissé products
accepted to hundreds of
new retail accounts, sold
in 500 stores nationwide

December 2013
Angel round of $500k
closed, approval from
investors to
over-subscribe

April 2014
Cissé cocoa accepted
by Kroger region: trial
for national roll-out

December 2014
Cissé closes its
$1.25mm over-
subscribed Series A
round of funding

March 2015
Super Thins unveiled at
Natural Foods Expo
West tradeshow and
initial orders received

March 2015
Cissé given a NEXTY
award at Expo for the
innovation of a
traceable supply chain

June 2015
Super Thins approved
by BJ's for front of club
placement in all 150+
clubs

June 2015
First Target purchase
order received for 600
locations

September 2015
Super Thins launch on
Amazon, on shelf in
New Seasons, Kings
Market (NY, NJ, CT)
JFK Terminals 4&5 and
many other locations

8

Where are we going: plan for continued growth

Cissé gained national distribution in premier retailers such as Whole Foods and by
category leaders such as Kroger, Target, and BJ's Wholesale Club

9

How do we hit topline goal: Super Thins

- Launched September 2015 with initial sell through at 4x expectations
- Super food toppings: cashews, coconut, cranberries, pepitas, cherries
- Non-GMO Verification in progress for 2016
- On trend: The inclusion of "natural ingredients" is the #1 attribute consumers look for when purchasing a snack[1]

1. Mintel - The Snacking Occasion (2014)

10

Why brownie thin cookies: competitive landscape

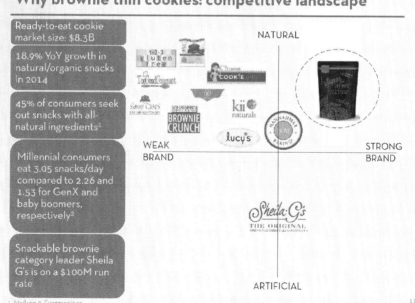

Ready-to-eat cookie market size: $8.3B

18.9% YoY growth in natural/organic snacks in 2014

45% of consumers seek out snacks with all-natural ingredients[1]

Millennial consumers eat 3.05 snacks/day compared to 2.26 and 1.53 for GenX and baby boomers, respectively[2]

Snackable brownie category leader Sheila G's is on a $100M run rate

1. Neilsen 2. Euromonitor

11

59

What's our edge: giving the consumer a better option

Like many other packaged food companies with big exits, Cissé is positioning itself as a better-for-you version of an existing consumer favorite

12

Who's making it all happen: the team

Motivated and experienced team driving topline sales growth

Diana Lovett, FOUNDER
7+ years experience international business and development
Successfully managed multi-million dollar infrastructure projects in emerging markets
M.A. from Cambridge and a B.A. from Yale

Kelsey Byrne, CHIEF FINANCIAL OFFICER
3 years at Morgan Stanley in asset backed credit
M.B.A. from Tuck School of Business and B.A. from Dartmouth College

Kelsey Hopping, DIRECTOR OF MARKETING
5 years experience at top advertising agencies including Crispin Porter + Bogusky and mcgarrybowen; Brands include Ben & Jerry's and HONEST Tea

Rachael Styer, DIRECTOR OF SALES
Highly successful at growing in-store sales
B.A. from Yale University in Environmental Studies

Abby Harrison, OPERATIONS MANAGER
Prior roles include QA and Operations at Temple Turmeric and Red Jacket Orchards
B.S. at Cornell University in Food Science and Operations Management

13

Who is helping: deeply committed board & advisors

Industry leaders who are passionate about the products and company's success

Gigi Lee Chang
Founder, Plum Organics

Marc Shedroff
VC, Google, Samsung

Angela Hockman
Comptroller, WikiFoods
Formerly at Food Should Taste Good,
Yasso

Kellee Joost
Managing Director,
Golden Seeds

Greg Lagios
Director of Business Development at Half
Pops, former VP of Sales at Food Should
Taste Good and Angie's Popcorn

Steve White
Former Global VP
Cookies & Crackers,
Pepperidge Farms

Amanda Barrasso
Operations, The Chia Co
Formerly at Food Should Taste Good

Mike Watts
Director of Marketing, Yasso
Formerly at Stirrings, Food
Should Taste Good

14

Questions? Contact us!

Diana Lovett
dlovett@cissetrading.com

Kelsey Byrne
kbyrne@cissetrading.com

15

Notes

32630962R00036

Made in the USA
Middletown, DE
11 June 2016